Earth's Changing Surface and Natural Resources

 HOUGHTON MIFFLIN HARCOURT

Printed in Mexico

ISBN: 978-0-544-07318-0

6 7 8 9 10 0908 21 20 19 18 17 16

4500608014   A B C D E F G

Be an Active Reader!

Look at these words.

weathering	**humus**	natural resource
erosion	**bedrock**	renewable resource
deposition	**soil horizon**	nonrenewable resource
sediment	**soil profile**	conservation
soil		

Look for answers to these questions.

What kinds of changes happen to Earth's surface?

What is weathering?

What does erosion do?

What happens during deposition?

How does water shape and move rock?

How does ice shape and move rock?

What does wind do to rock?

How does soil form?

What kinds of soil are there?

How is soil arranged in layers?

How does soil gain or lose health?

Why are natural resources important?

What are renewable resources?

What are nonrenewable resources?

How can we conserve resources?

What kinds of changes happen to Earth's surface?

If you looked out the window this morning, you probably didn't see Earth changing. When most people think about changes to Earth, they think about big, sudden changes like earthquakes and volcanoes.

Actually, Earth changes all the time, slowly, in tiny amounts. Hills rise up and wear down. Rivers cut through the land. Ice and wind change rock. These kinds of changes are interesting to geologists, scientists who study the earth. Over thousands or millions of years, these slow changes can have a big impact on our world.

The Grand Canyon is the result of the action of the water in the river, wind on the cliffs, and the land around it pushing upward.

What is weathering?

Look at the photograph below. This is a natural bridge. It was not built by human beings. This bridge was formed by weathering. Weathering is the breaking down of rocks on Earth's surface into smaller pieces. Water, wind, ice, and gravity can all cause weathering. So can plants, animals, and chemicals.

Water causes weathering when it freezes inside cracks in rocks. When water freezes, it expands. The expansion makes the cracks larger. If freezing and expansion happen enough times, the rocks will break.

When gravity causes rocks to fall on other rocks, that's weathering. Another type of weathering occurs when wind-blown sand collides with rocks.

Natural Bridge, in Virginia, was formed when weathered rock collapsed.

Animals can cause weathering when they dig in the soil. Digging can expose rocks to water and wind.

Plants cause weathering when their roots enter tiny cracks in rocks. As the roots grow, the cracks expand. If the plants keep growing, the rocks may split. Soft plant roots can break rocks!

Chemicals in water also cause weathering. The chemicals combine with rocks and change them so that they break easily. This type of weathering—from rivers, streams, or rain—is called chemical weathering.

The white covering on this stone lion in the city of Leeds, England, is an effect of chemical weathering from acid rain. Acid rain is precipitation mixed with chemicals from air pollution and other sources.

What does erosion do?

Weathering is not the only change that rocks on Earth go through. Rocks can undergo erosion. Erosion is the process of moving weathered rock from one place to another. Erosion sometimes moves large boulders great distances.

Suppose a river flows down a mountain. The rushing water can move large rocks and weather them into smaller rocks and gravel. The smaller rocks and gravel that have moved downstream have been eroded.

Weathering and erosion happen over a long period of time. Wearing down a rock may take thousands of years.

The rocks beside this river won't stay there forever. Over time, water will weather and erode them.

What happens during deposition?

Keep thinking about the mountain river that weathers and erodes rocks. How far can a river keep moving pieces of rock? After all, rock is heavier than water, so the pieces should sink.

The river is able to carry the pieces because the river is moving fast. When the water slows enough, it can no longer carry the pieces. They fall to the bottom of the riverbed or at the side of the river.

When moving water, wind, or ice drops a piece of rock, sand, or earth, this process is called deposition. The small pieces that are deposited are called sediment. Sediment can pile up in layers. The top layers and the water press on the lower layers and turn them into new rock.

Soft ground, such as mud on river banks, is often the result of deposition.

The sand on this beach came from eroded rock.

How does water shape and move rock?

Imagine a river that is flowing down a gentle slope. This water erodes small rocks, gravel, and sand. At a curve, the river weathers the rock on its outside bank. It deposits sand on the inside bank. Over many years, the erosion and deposition can change the course of the river.

Erosion also occurs on ocean shores. Powerful waves crash on cliffs and over time weather the cliff rock. The weathered rock crumbles into the sea in pieces. The pieces become pebbles and sand. The sand and pebbles sink to the ocean floor or perhaps collect on beaches.

How does ice shape and move rock?

The Great Lakes are five huge bodies of water on the border between the United States and Canada. These lakes were dug by moving ice.

Thousands of years ago, much of North America and Europe was covered by sheets of ice called glaciers. During cold winters, the glaciers moved forward. They picked up large boulders. The bottoms of the glaciers and the boulders scraped the ground. This scraping left holes, which filled with water when the temperature rose. The filled holes were new lakes. Thousands of lakes in the northern part of the United States were formed this way.

When the temperature drops, more water at the front of a glacier freezes, and the glacier advances.

What does wind do to rock?

Wind can carry grains of sand and other solids that wear away rock. When the wind blows against the rock, particles bang into the rock. Over thousands or millions of years, that action can sculpt the rock into new forms.

Wind can also deposit the sand that it carries. When wind keeps dropping sand in one place, a sand dune forms. Wind then shapes the dune. The wind lifts sand from one side of the dune and drops it on the other side. When the sand keeps shifting in the same direction, the dune advances over the land.

A sand dune in a desert may move as much as 10 meters (33 feet) in one year.

Whether you like worms or not, they play a crucial role in forming soil, which grows food.

How does soil form?

As rock weathers and erodes, it breaks into smaller and smaller pieces. Over a long time, the pieces become small enough to form soil. Soil gives us almost everything we eat. Plants grow in soil, and animals eat those plants.

Soil is a mixture. It contains tiny bits of rock, humus, water, and air. Humus is the remains of decaying plants and animals. Humus provides nutrients for growing plants. Earthworms loosen and mix the soil. This allows air and water into the soil, which are used by plants.

What kinds of soil are there?

Soil forms best in temperate climates. Temperate places freeze for part of the year and are warm or hot for part of the year. The freezing, melting, and refreezing of water in cracks in rock weather the rock. Rain in temperate places weathers rock, too. Weathering is slower in dry climates and in climates where ice doesn't often melt.

When iron is in rock, the resulting soil is red.

Soil forms better on flat land and in valleys. On mountains, rain and melting ice carry weathered rock downhill, so the soil is thin at the top.

The properties of soil include color, texture, the ability to hold water, and the ability to support plant growth. The color of soil depends on the kind of rock it came from and the kinds of minerals that made up the rock.

Scientists classify soils by their texture. A soil's texture comes from the size of its particles. Sand has the largest particles, making a coarse texture. Silt is similar to sand, but its particles are smaller. Both sand and silt are carried and deposited by moving water. Clay has even finer particles.

The type of soil affects how well plants grow. Sandy soils aren't very rich. They contain little humus, and water passes through them quickly. Clay-rich soils contain little air. They are packed too closely for many plant roots to grow. A third type of soil is loamy. It contains sand, silt, clay, and lots of humus. It is dark brown in color. It holds water during dry periods. Loamy soils support a wide variety of plant growth.

> Sandy, clay-rich, and loamy soils form in different places and in different ways.

sandy

clay-rich

loamy

How is soil arranged in layers?

Soil has three main layers. The soil that you've seen and felt is the top layer, the topsoil. Topsoil has the most humus, air, and water. It's where plants put their roots.

The next layer down is subsoil. It is made of clay and weathered rock. It contains lots of minerals. Water carries minerals down from the topsoil into the subsoil. These add to the minerals already in the subsoil's clay and rock.

topsoil

subsoil

bedrock

The bottom layer is bedrock. Bedrock is solid rock. If erosion or an earthquake uncovers bedrock, it can break down to become soil.

Each of the three layers forms a soil horizon. The soil layers atop each other form a soil profile. Scientists study soil profiles to see how healthy the soil in an area is.

Windbreaks keep wind from blowing away soil. Farmers plant rows of trees to block the wind.

How does soil gain or lose health?

Healthy soil is important to farmers. There are many things that can threaten a soil's health. Plants use up the nutrients in soil. Wind can blow soil away, and rain can wash it away.

Farmers use crop rotation to keep nutrients in soil. They plant different crops in the same field in different years. For example, beans add nitrogen to the soil. Corn removes it. So farmers plant corn one year and beans another.

Intercropping also helps keep soil healthy. Intercropping is planting more than one kind of plant in the same field at the same time.

Contour plowing also improves soil. Plowing along soil's natural curves helps keep rain from washing the soil away.

Why are natural resources important?

Soil is a natural resource, a material found in nature that people use. Other natural resources that we use are air and water. We need these natural resources to live. Humans aren't the only ones who use natural resources. Animals and plants need air and water, too. Animals and plants are also natural resources for humans. We rely on them for food.

Sunlight and wind are two other natural resources. Sunlight helps plants grow. Wind helps spread seeds to grow more plants. We can also use sunlight and wind to provide electrical energy.

These natural resources provide materials for furniture, clothes, and bedding.

What are renewable resources?

A natural resource that can be replaced in a reasonable amount of time is called a renewable resource. Sunlight, air, water, and wind are renewable resources. Animals and people remove oxygen from the air when they breathe, but plants put oxygen back in. We use water, but water also becomes water vapor. Water vapor forms clouds, and rain from clouds provides us with more water. Plants and trees are two other renewable resources. We can use them, but we can also grow more.

We must use our renewable resources wisely. If forests are cut down too quickly, we may not be able to plant trees fast enough to replace them. If we use poor farming methods, the soil may become too thin to grow crops.

New trees in this forest have been planted to replace the trees that were cut down.

What are nonrenewable resources?

A natural resource that cannot be replaced in a reasonable amount of time is called a nonrenewable resource. Once we use up the supply of a nonrenewable resource, we can't get any more.

Fossil fuels are one type of nonrenewable resource. Fossil fuels include oil, natural gas, and coal. Oil is made into gasoline for cars, trucks, and buses. Coal is used to make electricity.

Fossil fuels come from the remains of living things from long ago. When those living things died, they decayed and sank into the ground. Over millions of years, they changed into different materials. Plants were pressed into a hard solid form, or coal. Very small living things turned into oil and natural gas.

Coal is one kind of fossil fuel. Once all fossil fuels are used up, we'll need to find other kinds of fuel.

Copper comes from ore that is mined. Pennies are coated with copper.

Most metals are nonrenewable. These include copper, tin, aluminum, nickel, gold, and silver. Earth contains a limited amount of each metal, and there is less today than there used to be.

Metals are important. Copper is used in electrical wires and many machines. Silver is used in jewelry and in industry. Aluminum is a major part of cars.

We may run out of some metals and fossil fuels during our lifetime. We must learn to use these resources wisely.

How can we conserve resources?

If we don't want to run out of resources, we must use conservation. Conservation is the use of less of something in order to make it last longer.

Although water is renewable, some parts of the United States don't have enough water. We can conserve water by using less of it. One way is to take shorter showers.

Reusing is also a way to conserve. You can find new ways to use old products, or you can keep using products longer.

Recycling is also conservation. In your home, you might recycle glass, plastic, paper, and metal.

If your school doesn't have a recycling program, work with a teacher and other students to start one.

People build houses from old glass bottles and plastic bottles!

People and companies recycle and reuse materials to make some really interesting things. Recycled rubber tires can become handbags. An empty warehouse can become apartments. Reusing the warehouse building conserves materials that would be needed to build a new building.

Electronic items such as computers and phones contain metals that can be recycled. Companies that make these items and the stores that sell them often recycle them.

Conservation is important to Earth's future.

Responding

Investigate Soil

With a shovel, take a sample of the soil near you. Put it in a jar, and label it with the place where you found it. Record your observations. What is its color and texture? What kind of soil do you think it is? What materials of different sizes do you see? Can you see any living things in it? How well does it hold water? Based on where you found it, how well does this soil support plant growth? If possible, go to one or two places that have different types of soil. Take samples at each one and compare the samples.

Show a Rock's Story

Using information from this book, create a poster that explains weathering, erosion, and deposition. On your poster, include a diagram that explains each process. Include photos or drawings with captions in your diagram. Your photos or drawings should help you to explain how rock is worn away and moved to other places.

Glossary

bedrock [BED·rahk] Solid rock found under soil.

conservation [kahn·ser·VAY·shun] The use of less of something to make its supply last longer.

deposition [dep·uh·ZISH·uhn] The dropping or settling of eroded materials.

erosion [uh·ROH·zhuhn] The process of moving weathered rock and sediment from one place to another.

humus [HYOO·muhs] The remains of decayed plants or animals in the soil.

natural resource [NACH·er·uhl REE·sawrs] A material found in nature that people and other living things use.

nonrenewable resource [nahn·rih·NOO·uh·buhl REE·sawrs] A natural resource that cannot be replaced in a reasonable amount of time.

renewable resource [rih•NOO•uh•buhl REE•sawrs] A natural resource that can be replaced within a reasonable amount of time.

sediment [SED•uh•ment] Sand, bits of rock, fossils, and other matter carried and deposited by water, wind, or ice.

soil [SOYL] A mixture of water, air, tiny pieces of rock, and humus.

soil horizon [SOYL huh•RIZ•uhn] A layer of soil with different physical characteristics from the layer of soil above it and the layer of soil below it.

soil profile [SOYL PRO•fyl] A cross-section of soil that shows the various layers of soil.

weathering [WETH•er•ing] The breaking down of rocks on Earth's surface into smaller pieces.